Poems for a Winter's Night

A Poetry Collection

by

C. D. Melley

Poems for a Winter's Night

Poems for a Winter's Night
Copyright © 2015 by C. D. Melley

Published by Douglas J. McLeod

Cover Photo: "Sunlight on the hoar frost (painting by
Arkhip Kuindzhi, 1876-1890)" By Arkhip
Kuindzhi (1842-1910)
(http://kuinje.ru/kuinji_kartina5.php) [Public
domain], via Wikimedia Commons

First Paperback Edition: 2015

ISBN: 978-0993773235
ISBN-10: 0993773230

10 9 8 7 6 5 4 3 2 1

To my darling Catherine,
with much love.

Other Poetry Books Written by C. D. Melley

Slammin' on the Rails

Missing You

There is a distinct chill in the air
My coffee cup is empty
And, the silence in the room
Is deafening.

I think back to the last time we were together
On that warm summer night
And, those memories
Bring a warmth to my soul.

However, many months have gone
Since those August moments
And, my bed has grown cold
Without you lying beside me.

I still long for the day
When we'll be together again
Knowing how much
You complete me.

There is a hole in my heart
Because I miss you, terribly
But, I'm still counting down the days
Until we're reunited again.

Polar Vortex

There is a bitter cold
Gripping the continent
Temperatures are unseasonably low
Everywhere you go.

Normally warm climates in the South
Now have forced people to switch
From t-shirts to sweaters
An unwelcome change in attire.

And, people traditionally used to the weather
Are bundled up even more.
School days have been cancelled
Not wanting to risk the health of young students.

They will rejoice for an extra day from their studies
While parents dread the extra distraction
Indoor activities will be on the agenda
But, how much of *Frozen*, can one endure?

For me, I can take solace
In a hot cup of coffee
But, knowing I, too, will need to venture out
eventually
Work never stops for us adults.

Fire on Ice

The skaters take their positions
Close to one another
The anticipation is mounting
As they ready for their performance.

The music starts to play
And, they dance to the beat
They move and jump on the ice
Impressing the crowd in attendance.

Their act is filled with drama
As their moves tell a story
A frozen tango filled with passion
That melts the coldest heart.

They finish their dance
And earn the applause from the crowd
But, they wait with baited breath
Seeking final approval.

Their marks come in
And they are overjoyed
Perfect scores across the board
And a golden story has been told.

Banging the Drums

There was a song once
Where the troubadour sang
He didn't want to go to work
He wanted to bang on the drum all day.

Funny how life imitates art
For thanks to a Christmas gift
I now own a personal
Desktop drum set.

I'll admit I'm not much of a percussionist
I have no sense of rhythm
But, there have been moments
Where I've tried to break out into a solo.

I'll admit I'm no Lars Ulrich
Hell, I'm no Sheila E
But, sometimes when I'm alone
I bust a beat for me.

Alas, work comes a-callin'
And, I have to put my sticks down
But, next time it's quiet at my place
I'll grab the sticks and go to town.

Relapse

I don't know what came over me
I couldn't help myself
But, now here I am
Back at square one.

The bright lights beckoned
As did the familiar chime
They called out to me
To return once more.

Some people might say it was caused by stress
Others say I wanted to go back
Regardless of the reason
The allure was too tempting for me.

With a scratch of the latex
Later by a push of a button
And 20 months of recovery
Went down the drain.

So, here I am
Back at square one
One day at a time
I start the Road to Recovery again.

Loss of Time

I said I was only going out for an hour
I had a plan in place
Alas, my intentions
Were never followed to the letter.

I wanted to go out for some fun
Get my mind off my troubles
But, the troubles found me
And, distracted my thoughts.

One became two
Two became four
The hours ticked away
I lost track of the score.

It was half past three
When I made it back
I had a lot of explaining to do
As to why I lost track.

I have learned my lesson
Next time set an alarm
So I can be more punctual
And, do myself less harm.

Vacation to Hell

I think coming here
Was a mistake I made
I had all good intentions
But, they didn't turn out like I hoped.

The problem started when I checked-in
And, my card was not valid
I had to pay a deposit
An additional $100 gone.

And, I needn't mention
My long night out
A vice revisited
Another $110 down the toilet.

Throw in less than 3 hours sleep
Not consecutive time at the least
Thank God I found a coffee shop
My one solace this trip.

My train leaves soon
And, I can return home
But, only to return
To my usual routine in the morn.

Bitter Cold

The mercury has plummeted
The winds howl in the air
It's not safe for anyone to be out
On this chilly day.

They're forecasting temperatures
In the minus teens Celsius
Just below 0 on the Fahrenheit scale
Frostbite can be imminent.

On days like today
It's best to take shelter
But, for those who must go out
It's an unwelcome adventure.

A hot beverage should be in order
Coffee, tea, or hot chocolate
Whatever will warm up
A shivering soul today.

The groundhog said there'd be
Six more weeks of this.
I'm starting to wonder
How appetizing rodent really is?

Unhinged

You try to lead me astray
With your seductive ways
Even when you know
I'm happily in a relationship.

You've fed me lies
Appealing to my compassionate soul
In hopes I'd leave my current love
For you.

And, even when we did talk
You told me to keep it from her
Another concoction
In your web of deceit.

You're certifiable
Trying to get what you want
There is no stopping you
In your quest.

Can't you get it through your head
I'm in love with someone else?
But, your crazy eyes and lies
Will forever cloud your judgment.

Valentine's Apart

It's that time of year again
When love fills the air
And, couples share their devotion
Towards one another.

Fortunes have been spent
On flowers, candy, and cards
An industry in itself
Promoting the day of l'amour.

Alas, I am spending this day
Miles away from the woman I adore
She shares the same sentiment
That I cannot be with her.

However, I've made a vow
To change things from hereon in
To be with the one I love
On February 14th's in the future.

I sent her a card
Along with a special surprise
The papers she's been waiting for
Telling her I'm coming 'home'.

Family Day

A special holiday was created
A few years ago
A day meant to be spent with loved ones
To enjoy with one another.

Many spend it on outings
Out on a February day
Fun activities abound
For parents and children to enjoy.

However, I have no children of my own
To spend this day with
The hours were well spent
Doing household chores.

But, I must admit
I like a day off from work
Although, I'm dreading
What's waiting for me at my desk.

So, I decide to make the most of it
Enjoying some spare time
Pulling out a quill and some paper
And, writing a few rhymes.

The Native Game

Most people of my land
Believe the National sport involves ice and skates
However, while that is partially true
There is another that makes the claim.

They, too, involve sticks
But with a webbed pocket instead of a blade
A rubber ball replaces the puck
And, the surface is green or gray instead of white.

During the summer months
The game is played on grass
When the weather turns colder
A modified hockey rink is the field of play.

The action is fast-paced
Shots whiz by with great speed
And the hacks and hits are just as hard
As a bodycheck from an enforcer.

They call the game 'lacrosse'
And, it's an exciting thrill
More goals abound than in hockey
And, it's a game around as long as this land.

The Hype of Smut

I know of the adage
'Sex sells'
But, I don't understand
Why this is the case?

Erotica seems to dominate
The literary landscape
And people are flocking to movie theatres
To see a retelling of one of the most popular.

I get that it's all a fantasy
An escape from one's normal life
However, I have to wonder
If some of the lines have blurred.

I know I shouldn't judge
Because that would make me a hypocrite
Since I, too, have written erotica
Under another persona.

So, erotic fantasies are the new fad
Nothing wrong with that, I guess
But, in my opinion, there's no replacing
True love with another person.

Our Fur Babies

The looks on their faces
Are so adorable
Whenever I see them
Over my Skype feed.

One is an adorable Pomeranian
Who is the epitome of cuteness
My love says I'd be wrapped around the pup's finger
And, I wholeheartedly agree.

The other is a sweet little Yorkie
Whose tongue hangs out of his mouth
But, is endearing in his own right
A 'son' to call my own.

We both know we won't be able
To have human children in our lives
Too much stress and aggravation
For our psyches to bear.

However, we are proud parents
Of two wonderful fur babies
Rescued dogs from previous owners
A loving home they've found with us.

Coffee or Tea

There are two different hot beverages
Writers enjoy while dating their muse
Both provide ample fuel
Towards their inspiration.

Some people enjoy the bean
A strong hit of caffeine to their system
I admit I am one of those
Who perks up with a warm brew.

However, I am also a fan
Of steeping leaves and twigs
A bevy of varieties adorn my pantry
To tantilize my exotic tastebuds.

Sometimes it's hard to decide
What I prefer to get my words flowing
Do I brew, or do I steep?
A quandary for my day of creativity.

I throw caution to the wind
And grab my mug of choice
On this cold day I choose neither
And opt for a serving of hot cocoa.

A Friend in Need

I sit here working on my craft
My muse is in overdrive
Then, my cellphone rings
And, for once, I answer the call.

The voice on the other end
Is a dear friend of mine
A fellow sister in recovery
Wanting someone to talk to.

She tells me of her weekend
And, of how the vice attempted to creep in again
She asked for some guidance
As to handle the situation.

I tell her to remain vigilant
And not give in to the temptation
Because, if we let our guards down
We will slip back into the Dark World again.

After some reassurance not to go back
We share the fruits of our craft
A wonderful conversation
Between two addicts back on track.

Peer Pressure

Yes, I know I messed up
I own up to my mistake
But, my bretheren are now accusing me
That I'm falling back into the illness.

They say I'm turning into
'A compulsive slipper'
Twice in a month
Raises alarm bells for them.

I know I have work to do
In order to right my ship
However, I've never been one
Who likes being ordered what to do.

I don't mind asking for guidance
When I feel I need it
Is this one of those times? Absolutely
And, I need to do it on my own terms.

I see they're doing it
To give me the kick in the butt I need
But, if they continue their hounding
It might force me back to my vice.

Annual Temptation

Anyone who knows me
Knows my affection for the bean
But, one retailer in particular
Is my preferred supplier.

It's a retailer renowned
Across the country
With a few pockets south of the border
Where its wares are available.

However, every February
Said store runs a promotion
Where customers are enticed with prizes
Earned by a roll of their rim.

I have given into the temptation
In years gone by
Alas, because of my addiction
Participating is forbidden.

It's tough to avoid
The bright red contest cups
But, if I want continued recovery
I must not give into my vice.

One Certain Thing

They say there are two things
That are certain in life
One seems more predominant
At this time of year.

While logic would dictate
It involves papers due in April
My financial pronouncements
Are not what I speak of.

The other option leads
To the act of mourning
But, death is far from
The emotions I feel.

The certain thing I speak of
Is how I feel for you
And the love within my heart
Is an emotion like no other.

You make my world
And, that is a feeling like no other
That is why our love
Will endure forever.

Beaming Uncle

I remember when my sister
Gave birth to my niece
And, the emotions that came through me
Were unlike any I ever felt before.

To see that little bundle of joy
For the first time
My family grew larger
And, a new title was bestowed upon me.

I have since been blessed
With another niece and three nephews
However, I confess I've been absent
In my relations with them.

But, my roommate has since been blessed
With a niece of his own
While they're a nation apart
I can see him overflowing with pride.

I hope he can learn
From the mistakes I've made
The title of 'Uncle'
Is one that should not be taken for granted.

Bothersome Back

I try to get comfortable
Sitting in my recliner
But, my back is acting up
Making me fidget in my seat.

I'm not sure if it's a pulled muscle
Or, even a slipped disc
The only thing I do know
Is that it's making me uncomfortable.

I could pop a couple of back pills
In hopes it'll alleviate the pain
However, I'm concerned
It might become habit-forming.

I should lie down
And, try to stretch it out
But, I have a full day ahead
Work looms on my schedule.

So, I'm forced to deal
With the crick in my lower back
Living through the pain
Because chiropractors are expensive.

Pancake Day

There is one Tuesday of the year
My friends and I look forward to
And, it is a day
That tantilizes our tastebuds.

Fried rounds of batter
Adorn the griddle
We ready the bottles of syrup
And, little pats of butter.

We fill our plates with the cakes
Adding our condiments as we go
We take in the aroma
Of our culinary creations.

My friends and I dive in
Scarfing back our meal
Savouring each bite
As it touches our palate.

We admit we love pancakes
And, we know we can enjoy them year-round
But, on this Shrove Tuesday
They taste extra special.

Winter Flooding

With the constant ebb and flow
Of the mercury in the thermometer
It does a number
On our aging infrastructure.

The underground pipes
Freeze and break
Causing copious amounts of water
To fill our streets.

With the chilling temperatures
The rushing aqua freezes
Making the roads above
Treacherous to navigate.

In some instances
Cars get frozen in their place
The flooding becoming solid
Around the base of their tires.

It's a nightmare on the roads
Of our city when they force
The subways to close
Making me wish
The Spring thaw comes soon.

Out On the Roads

The winds howl
And, the snow blows
But, for the lonely courier
He still has to make his delivery

He traverses the city
In all weather conditions
Making pick-ups as he goes
Where his dispatcher sends him.

He often debates
If it is all worth it
Making a commission of 40 dollars a day
For his troubles.

He knows it's miniscule
Compared to a normal minimum wage
He often wonders
If it's all worth it in the end.

Then, he remembers
What waits for him in the future
So, he soldiers on
Saving towards a new life down south.

www.ingramcontent.com/pod-product-compliance
Lightning Source LLC
Chambersburg PA
CBHW060552030426
42337CB00019B/3523